A PRACTICAL GUIDE

AS KINGS IN

Finding Your Place on *Your Kingdom Mountain*

Designed for Study or Group Discussion

BEN R. PETERS

Finding Your Place on Your Kingdom Mountain

Published by
KINGDOM SENDING CENTER
P. O. Box 25
Genoa, IL 60135

www.kingdomsendingcenter.org
ben.peters@kingdomsendingcenter.org

ISBN: 978-0-9789884-4-9

Cover design and book interior by *www.ChristianBookDesign.com*

Contents

Introduction

Before studying this book we strongly advise that you first read the book, *Kings and Kingdoms.* If you do not have access presently to that book, please read the following summary of the basic tenets of *Kings and Kingdoms.*

- Jesus has made us to be kings and priests unto Him (Revelation 1:6).
- Kings are not really kings until they have a kingdom.
- Most earthly kings in Bible times were subject to a "king of kings" or emperor.
- God needs us to fulfill administrative roles as kings over parts of His Kingdom on the earth.
- The more kings serving Him, the greater is His Kingdom.
- Our job as regional kings is to bring in resources for the King of Kings and expand His Kingdom.
- We are also called to serve, to bring justice and protection, and to provide opportunity for people to thrive and prosper.
- God wants us to rule on one or more of the seven mountains of society.
- We are not only to rule, but to raise up sons and daughters as princes and princesses, and prepare them so that they can also rule and reign.

- Our goal is not for personal advantage but for the purpose of spreading God's Kingdom.
- Only the humble can be trusted with high level authority at the top of these mountains.
- Many prophets are being raised up to anoint the new kings who will bring reformation, righteousness and justice on the earth.

The above bullet points will help you understand what you are about to read, but I highly recommend that you also read *Kings and Kingdoms* to get the most out of this guide to finding your place on God's mountain.

Chapter One

Defusing the Land Mines in Your Path

If you believe, as I do, that God has called you to a high calling as a "king" with a "kingdom", you will surely want to fulfill that glorious calling and take advantage of every divine appointment to position yourself for a promotion from Heaven. It would be foolish to ignore or turn down the King of Kings who wants to establish you in a place of great influence and impact.

As a person who loves the only One who could forgive your sins and prevent your eternal damnation, you surely want to fulfill the command of Jesus to "Seek first His Kingdom," by using your position to expand His Kingdom on the earth. Your goal is to bring as much of Heaven to earth as possible. Jesus taught us to pray, "Your Kingdom come, Your will be done, on earth as it is in Heaven." The more influence and impact you have on the earth, the more you will be able to fulfill this prayer.

Every journey has its unique challenges and your journey to a higher place on the mountain is no exception. The enemy who fears your climb up the mountain will try to make the pathway as dangerous and difficult as possible. He will go before you to plant land mines in places you least expect them. You need to identify and defuse these dangerous threats as efficiently as possible and continue your upward progress. Let's look briefly at two of the most common and difficult land mines that almost every Christian finds threatening his or her pathway to promotion.

I. NEGATIVE FEELINGS ABOUT YOURSELF

Even if you had been born into a family with two perfect parents, perfect siblings and perfect friends, I believe that you would still struggle through life with feelings of inadequacy and insecurity. You would feel inferior to others, guilty for your failures and fear that others will be disappointed in you. You would be concerned about your future life after death and you would struggle with many other emotions related to who you are as compared to who you thought you should be.

Why do I believe this? I believe it simply because you were born into a world that has been impacted by sin and the curse of Genesis 3:17. Until you have found yourself in the loving arms of your Savior and have received strong assurance from Him, you will feel deep down in your inner man that you are lacking something. This feeling of emptiness makes you feel insecure and unworthy.

Most of your life you have been fighting against your inner fears, emotional struggles and multiplied accusations from your enemy that you are a bad person, a total failure, and certainly not worthy to be loved by God or by anyone else. Your many efforts to make friends and to work hard to be successful are all subconscious attempts to disprove the self-condemning inner voices from your own spirit and from the spirit of darkness which seeks to destroy your soul. Even when you seem to be making progress to disprove these voices, one little negative comment from someone can put you in turmoil and reinforce all the insecurities you have experienced over your lifetime.

All of these negative feelings about yourself are huge roadblocks and dangerous land mines on your upward journey to your place on your mountain. You could also compare these negative feelings to a Goliath obstructing your pathway. It is absolutely imperative that you deal a death blow to this giant standing in your way of ruling with Christ and influencing your world in the way your King of Kings desires.

The number one negative feeling most of us have is a feeling of unworthiness because of guilt and condemnation. Let me share some insights God has given us from His Word that will help you evict this and all other negative voices from the throne of your heart.

A. Your Negative Thoughts and Feelings are not God's

Read carefully the following Scripture passage from Isaiah 55. There is more to it than what meets the eye.

> [6]*Seek the Lord while He may be found. Call upon Him while He is near.*
>
> [7]*Let the wicked forsake his way, and the unrighteous man his thoughts; let him return to the Lord, and He will have mercy on him; and to our God For He will abundantly pardon.*
>
> [8]***For** my thoughts are not your thoughts, nor are your ways My ways, says the Lord.*
>
> [9]*For as the heavens are higher than the earth, so are My ways higher than your ways, and My thoughts than your thoughts.*
>
> *(Isaiah 55:6 – 9)*

Please notice the word "for", in verse 8. The word here means "because". This word connects verse 7 with verse 8. It is critical to understand the connection.

In verse 7, God is saying that he will have mercy and "abundantly" pardon. That means He will totally wipe our sin off the map and out of the records. It's not just a grudging pardon, but an abundant pardon. That means He gives even more pardon than we need or ask for.

Then verse 8 says that He will do this because His ways are not our ways, nor are His thoughts our thoughts. Verse 9 goes on to say that His ways and thoughts are so far apart, it's like the distance from earth to the ends of the universe.

Now back to the word "for". What God is clearly implying is that He will pardon in a way that is far greater than the way that man would pardon. This is extremely important and we must force this truth into our mind and then down into our heart. If we do, we will have power to decapitate the goliath in our life, called "unworthiness".

The obvious problem is that we automatically think that God thinks like we do. When someone offends us, we have a hard time forgiving them. If we do forgive them, we keep them at arm's length, fearful they will hurt us again. We may pardon them, as a president pardons prisoners, but they are still guilty in our minds.

Our minds cannot totally forget and forgive hurts. It's only by the power of the Holy Spirit that we can truly forgive and forget. And when we come to God after we have messed up, we automatically think that He will look at us the same way we look at others. We carry the consciousness that we have failed, even after we've asked for forgiveness. Often we ask for forgiveness many times for the same thing. We feel like we have to convince God that we are truly sorry.

In addition, we feel that in some way He expects us to suffer and to do penance before we are really forgiven. These normal emotional and psychological responses to God materialized in the church in the Dark Ages through the practices or doctrines of indulgences, penance and purgatory.

But God is virtually screaming out, "NO, NO, NO! THAT IS NOT THE WAY I AM. I am merciful, full of compassion and I ABUNDANTLY pardon. I am not like you. I am so different from you in this way. I totally forgive, and I totally forget. I know your weakness and have great compassion for you. I love you, desire you and want you close to me. I will not hold you at arm's length after you sin and confess. I will hold you tight and draw you right into my heart to feel my love and passion for you. Please come to me and discover the difference between My ways and the ways of man."

B. Jesus Demonstrated His Father's Ways and Thoughts

When I discovered the truth I am about to share, I was amazed that I had never seen it before and had never heard anyone else speak about it. It reveals God's incredible, amazing grace and verifies the Old Testament Scripture we just looked at.

Again, I invite you to read carefully the following passage from John 20.

> *[19]Then, the same day at evening, being the first day of the week, when the doors were shut where the disciples were assembled, for fear of the Jews, Jesus came and stood in the midst and said to them, "Peace be with you."*
>
> *[20]When He had said this, He showed them His hands and His side. Then the disciples were glad when they saw the Lord.*
>
> *[21]So Jesus said to them again, "Peace to you! As the Father has sent Me I also send you."*

To really understand this story, we must remember what had just taken place in the lives of the disciples. Jesus had been crucified and the disciples had forsaken their Commander-in-Chief in the heat of the battle. One of their number, Judas, had betrayed Jesus and hung himself. Peter, the obvious leader of the twelve, had denied that he even knew Jesus. When he heard the rooster crow, he wept in guilt and remorse.

The eleven disciples were fearful and full of guilt and condemnation. They had heard from others that Jesus had been raised from the dead, but their troubled minds could not accept the news. One may wonder if they really wanted Him to come back to life after they had failed Him so badly. What would He say to them? Would He forgive them or pronounce judgment on them?

When He miraculously appeared to them behind locked doors, Jesus spoke not one word of correction, criticism or condemnation. His very first word was the word, "Shalom", meaning peace, but so much more than peace. The word, "Shalom", means blessing, favor, health and prosperity as well as peace.

How would we respond to disciples that were committed to us and failed us the way the disciples had failed Jesus? Would our first words to them be "Shalom"? Would we not want to give them a little lecture or a little discipline before we reluctantly accepted their apology?

But Jesus simply showed them the scars in his hands and feet and side as further evidence that He was without any doubt their Master, the One who had been crucified. Then He spoke to them again. Once more, He said, "Shalom!"

But that's not all He said to them.

What Jesus said next was extremely significant. He did not put them on probation. He did not suggest penance or send them to purgatory. Jesus commissioned them and promoted them – yes, Jesus gave them a promotion they certainly didn't deserve.

Jesus had detailed two requirements for his disciples. Unless they did two things they were not worthy to be even a disciple, much less an apostle.

1. The first was to forsake everything and follow Him.
2. The second was to take up their cross and follow Him.

We know that the disciples had met the first requirement, but when it came to the second, they chose not to ask the Romans for more crosses. Instead they fled and forsook Jesus, thus disqualifying them from the status of disciple.

But Jesus totally and abundantly pardoned them and then promoted them to the status of apostle. When He said, "As the Father sent Me, so send I you", He was making them apostles. The word "apostle" means "sent one". The Father sent Jesus as His Apostle to the world, and Jesus likewise sent His disciples as apostles to the world.

In two statements, Jesus fully forgave and abundantly pardoned the eleven disciples and He gave them the same position that God had given Him on the earth. Then He breathed resurrection life into them and gave them incredible authority to represent Him in all the world.

My obvious point is simply this: If Jesus could so completely pardon and then immediately promote his disciples who had failed Him so badly, then He can also completely pardon you and promote you to your divine calling and destiny. Because you are called to promote His greater Kingdom by ruling over a part of it, you can and you must destroy the giant called "Unworthiness", through these and other promises and examples in the Word of God.

Feelings of Inferiority

In addition to feelings of guilt and condemnation, we may feel inadequate because we don't believe we are as gifted or talented as others. We may be a part of a racial minority or a poor family or not as intelligent or attractive as others. We may have a history of failure, rather than success. Does God address these issues in talking about leaders in the Kingdom? Yes, dear friend, He certainly does.

Paul addresses this issue head on in I Corinthians 1:26-31.

> [26]*For you see your calling, brethren, that not many wise according to the flesh, not many mighty, not many noble, are called.*
>
> [27]*But God has chosen the foolish things of the world to put to shame the wise, and God has chosen the weak things of the world to put to shame the things which are mighty;*
>
> [28]*And the base things of the world and the things which are despised God has chosen, and the things which are not, to bring to nothing the things that are,*
>
> [29]*That no flesh should glory in His presence.*
>
> [30]*But of Him you are in Christ Jesus, who became for us wisdom from God – and righteousness and sanctification and redemption,*
>
> [31]*That as it is written, "He who glories, let him glory in the Lord."*

So whether you feel foolish, weak, base, despised or a "nothing", God has a plan for you and God has chosen you for a high and holy calling.

I'm so sorry, but the apostle, Paul, just took away every excuse you ever had.

So let's agree to behead the ugly old giant called "Negative Feelings About Yourself."

PERSONAL CHECKUP TIME #1

1. What makes you feel the most inferior to others?

2. What would Jesus say to you about that?

3. What personal past failure makes you feel the most guilty?

4. What would Jesus tell you about your past failure?

5. Do other people close to you struggle with similar insecurities and guilt?

6. Do you know how to help them?

II. EMOTIONAL PAIN AND RESULTING PROBLEMS

Now let's take a quick look at a first cousin of "Negative Feelings About Yourself".

If you are a living, breathing human being, with the ability to read this print, you have already been wounded emotionally by a multitude of people and situations. The pain of these experiences produces certain subconscious responses to other life situations and relationships. These responses are usually very negative. They may even be total blind spots in your life. You may feel your responses are normal, but others may see them as rather abnormal.

On the other hand, your negative responses can be quite extreme and may greatly trouble you, but you have not found a way to overcome your reactions of anger, jealousy, fear, lust, self-pity, etc. But for you to be able to properly rule as a representative of the King of Kings, you need to be healed of past pain and you need to know how to properly process future pain in a biblical way.

Fortunately, God has been raising up ministries such as Elijah House Ministries, founded by John Sandford, that specialize in bringing freedom to your soul. Today, there are many different approaches to what is sometimes called deliverance or inner healing. One particularly effective approach is called Sozo, and is used by many, including Bethel Temple in Redding, California, a church pastored by Bill Johnson, who is one of our favorite Bible teachers.

One basic foundation principle of inner healing is that where there is fruit, there is a root. In other words, outward behavior has an inner cause. Unhealthy responses to situations are caused by pain from past experiences, which are often subconsciously triggered by fear of that pain being repeated.

Another principle is that the root is a root of bitterness. The person who received the pain tends naturally to judge the human that delivered the attack and subconsciously he or she feels bitterness towards that person. The inner healing specialist will try to help you recall experiences where you felt a particular type of pain, going back to your early childhood and in some cases all the way back to the womb. Science is confirming how much an unborn baby can feel the emotions of his or her mother and others close to her.

Some babies are born with a rejection complex because their parents did not want to have them. They can feel their parents' emotions and react to the tone of voice of those around them while they are developing in the womb. You might have been emotionally wounded before you remember anything in your childhood. But spiritually gifted and trained ministers of deliverance can help you discover the source of your pain. Then they can walk you through the process of forgiving and repenting for judging those who hurt you.

Yes, it's a two-step process. It's not enough to forgive them. You must also repent because you subconsciously judged them when they hurt you and God has given all judgment to Jesus (John 5:22). We are judged in the same way we judge others, so it's important to confess all judgments we have made against others. When you both forgive and repent, you can find healing and freedom from the affects of that pain.

In our ministry, we strongly advise everyone who serves on our team to both receive this healing ministry and to learn how to serve it to others. We need our people to work together in harmony and unity. Unresolved roots of bitterness create tension and conflict which create problems which we don't intend, bringing disunity and disharmony to the team.

Because we all have been hurt and wounded and we all have judged those who hurt us, we recommend that everyone gets professional help to get freedom from the fruit of their pain. Some people argue that Jesus took all of that pain on the cross and we don't need to go back and dig it up. Jesus paid the price for freedom, but sometimes we don't walk in it until we take the power of the cross back to the roots of our pain and deal with it. Until we confess our bitterness or judgment, we may continue to experience the fruit of the bitter root which is buried deep in our subconscious being.

As mentioned above, we also recommend that everyone possible learns enough about inner healing to help others find victory. Those who would rule with Christ must be servants of the people God has given them. Bringing spiritual and emotional freedom is one wonderful way to serve people. In addition, you will be helping train your people to help others, since their testimony of victory will inspire others to get help for themselves.

PERSONAL CHECKUP #2

1. Do you struggle to control any unwanted emotions?

2. Do you feel deep pain when certain people come to mind?

3. Have you ever before asked God to forgive you for judging people who have hurt you?

4. Do you need help to understand your pain and your reaction to it?

5. Do you know of anyone who can work with you to bring healing to your emotions?

Chapter Two

Your Vision is Too Small

After ministering one-on-one to thousands of individuals over several decades, it is my firm conviction that almost 100% of Christians have a vision that is smaller than God's vision for them. God knows how much He deposited into each of our lives and He has a special plan for each one of us that fits the gifts and talents He has given us.

Let me make some suggestions to enlarge your vision and expand your dream. As someone said, "It's better to shoot for the sun and reach the moon than to aim for nothing and hit it."

I. CHECK OUT SOME AMAZING RAGS-TO-RICHES CHARACTERS

The word of God is so full of stories of people who went from the ash heap to the throne. Cinderella has nothing on characters like Joseph, Ruth, David, Daniel and Esther in the Old Testament, and John the Baptist, Mary, Peter, Matthew, Paul and others in the New Testament who would have never been expected to accomplish what they did. In reading these stories, your faith will grow until you believe that if God did it for them, He can do it for you.

Take Joseph, for instance. He was a spoiled kid, hated by his ten older brothers. He was dropped into a pit, sold into slavery, thrown into prison and then forgotten by his friends there. In one amazing day, he went from the prison to the palace and became a "king" under Pharaoh, a king of kings.

Ruth was a Moabite widow, whose mother-in-law was leaving Moab to return to Israel. Ruth begged Naomi to allow her to go with her to Israel, where she would be a foreigner or a "minority" person with no real relatives or friends. She became a beggar just to keep from starving and ended up married to a wealthy young man. She then became a great grandmother to King David and her name will always be remembered as an ancestor of Jesus.

David had seven older brothers and they wouldn't give him the time of day. His father apparently didn't respect him that much either. When his talents and gifts were finally recognized, bringing him some temporary glory, King Saul tried to kill him. David had to hide in caves and Philistine cities. Even his own little band of men wanted to stone him when their camp was raided and plundered. David had a lot to overcome, but the day finally came when God put him on the throne of Judah and finally on the throne over all of Israel. In addition, as his kingdom grew, he eventually ruled over a number of other nations surrounding Israel.

Daniel was a captive slave in Babylon, but his faith in God and the Spirit of Revelation promoted him to a place next to the king of kings, Nebuchadnezzar. Even when others were jealous and had him thrown into the lions' den, God delivered him and gave him even greater honor.

Esther was also a captive slave, but God gave her great favor and she became the queen of the Persian Empire. Her influence changed the fate of the whole Jewish nation and preserved the seed of David through which Jesus Christ was born.

We could name so many more in both testaments, but you get the idea. Reading and meditating on God's Word will build your faith that God, who is no respecter of persons, can do the same for you.

II. READ AND MEDITATE ON THE PROMISES OF GOD

The Bible is filled with promises of God's love, grace and mercy. Many Scriptures declare that He helps the poor, lifts up the fallen and exalts the humble. Let's take a quick look at a few examples. Then you should do a treasure hunt of your own to find promises that relate to your dreams and desires.

Isaiah 60

> [1]*Arise, shine, for your light has come! And the glory of the Lord is risen upon you.*

Let's reword this verse and make it more personal.

> "I will arise and shine for MY light has come! And the glory of the Lord has risen upon ME."

> [2]*For behold, the darkness shall cover the earth, and deep darkness the people, but the Lord will arise over you, and His glory will be seen upon you.*

Let's reword again.

> "For behold, the darkness shall cover the earth, and deep darkness the people, but the Lord will arise over ME, and His glory will be seen upon ME."

If you continue through the chapter in this way, you will claim promises of great prosperity and blessing, honor, family unity and many other wonderful things. The most important blessing is found later in the chapter. God says that He will be with us and illuminate our world with His presence and glory.

The last verse of Isaiah declares this:

> [22]*A little one shall become a thousand, and a small one a strong nation. I, the Lord, will hasten it in its time.*

Think of that! God promises a one thousand fold multiplication. And a small one will become a strong nation. If we didn't have the examples in the Word that we have already referred to, we wouldn't understand what He was saying. Remember Abram, who had no children. Today, his seed includes not only the Jews, but all the Arabs as well. Remember little David (a small one), the outcast of the family. They called Jesus "the Son of David", which was meant to be a compliment to Jesus, but we know it was really a compliment to David.

Isaiah 61

I tell you saints, it just gets better and better. Chapter 61 starts out talking about our anointing:

> [1]*The Spirit of the Lord God is upon Me because He has anointed me to preach good tidings to the poor; He has sent Me to heal the brokenhearted, to proclaim liberty to the captives, and the opening of the prison to those who are bound.*

Yes, I know this referred to Jesus first of all, but Jesus said to His disciples, "As the Father has sent me, so send I you" (John 20:21). He also told us that we would do the same works that He did. (John 14:12).

Isaiah 61 goes on to prophesy incredible prosperity and favor and fame to the people of God.

> [6]*But you shall be named the priests of the Lord. They shall call you the servants of our God. You shall eat the riches of the Gentiles, and in their glory you shall boast.*

[7]Instead of your shame you shall have double honor. And instead of confusion they shall rejoice in their portion. Therefore in their land they shall possess double; everlasting joy shall be theirs.

[9]Their descendants shall be known among the Gentiles, and their offspring among the people. All who see them shall acknowledge them, that they are the posterity whom the Lord has blessed.

Can you put yourself into these Scriptures? If you can't, perhaps you need to go back to chapter one. You are one of God's children. He wants to bless you and use you to build His wonderful Kingdom to bless the whole earth. He wants to give you the privilege of helping Him take it back person by person from the clutches of the evil one.

III. CONSIDER SOME GREAT STORIES FROM MORE RECENT HISTORY

Gladys Aylward

Gladys Aylward, a London maid, with a clear call of God to missions, was told flat out by the head of the China Inland Mission that she was not qualified to be a missionary. Without anyone to send or support her, she saved all the money she could and travelled across Europe and Siberia, mostly by train. But she also had to walk some distance through the snow to the next city when the train stopped because of war between Russia and China. Then she had her passport stolen, forcing her to take a boat to Japan and finally to China. Her journey in China involved train, bus and mule to get to the city where an older lady was doing missionary work out of a traveler's inn.

The older lady lived only about eight months after Gladys' arrival and she was now on her own. Soon she began to work for the local government as a foot inspector enforcing the law against binding the feet of the young girls. Later the government used her to stop a bloody riot in a prison. Her greatest accomplishment may have been leading one hundred orphan children out of the war zone over a dangerous mountain pass during the Second World War. If you've never seen the classic movie, "Inn of the Sixth Happiness", I recommend it.

Has anyone ever told you that you were not qualified to pursue your God-given dream? It didn't stop Gladys Aylward and it shouldn't stop you.

Mother Teresa

Mother Teresa is much more famous, but she started in a similar way. She was told she couldn't do what God had called her to do. Her supervisors resisted her over and over again, but she would not take no for an answer. Finally, she was given the permission she requested. She began to minister to the poorest people in India. Her story is so amazing, and she has become a great hero to millions of Catholics, Protestants and non-Christians alike, winning a Nobel Peace Prize and becoming the subject of movies and great publicity.

Mother Teresa was just one little Catholic nun with a love for people, especially those whom no one else loved. Has God ever given you a burden for a certain group of people? You could be the next Mother Teresa or Gladys Aylward, unless of course, you are a guy and then you might want to be like our next example.

Abraham Lincoln

Abraham Lincoln was the son of uneducated parents and had only eighteen months of education himself. He taught himself by reading and studying on his own. He studied law books, became a lawyer and then ran for political office. Lincoln lost many elections, but he kept coming back and going to the next level in politics. He progressed from the Illinois House of Representatives to the Illinois Senate and then to the U.S. House of Representatives. From there, his zeal and strong convictions led him to run for president in 1860.

Lincoln developed a passion to free the slaves at a very young age. He made many speeches and proclaimed that America must become united on the issue of freedom for slaves. Although all of his support came from the north, he won the election and led the nation through one of its most turbulent times. Without Lincoln's passion and courage, America might be a much different nation today.

We could go on with story after story, but it's your turn to come up with your own.

PERSONAL CHECKUP TIME #3

1. Can you think of any other Bible characters, who defied the odds and became heroes of the faith?

2. Think about other people you know in history. If possible read a few biographies.

3. Who do you personally know that has been an example of coming from nowhere to make an impact on their world from the mountain God has given them? You might want to interview some respected leader and find out how he or she became the person of impact that they are today.

Chapter Three

A Desperate Need for Godly Kings

By the time you finish this chapter, I want you to be so convinced that God needs you ruling somewhere on some mountain that you will forget your limitations and give it everything you have for the sake of your King of Kings. He paid a high price to put you in a high place.

If God published an earthly newspaper, He would most likely have some interesting classified ads. I believe He would publish many *want ads* such as:

> WANTED: Kings to rule on the Education Mountain. Qualifications include love of children and youth, spiritual gifts of wisdom and knowledge, love of My creation and the history of My dealings with My creatures.

> WANTED: Kings to rule on the Government Mountain. Qualifications include a passionate desire to establish the Kingdom of Heaven on earth, an understanding of the principles of the Laws of God, a heart to serve God and country, and the ability to handle extremely tough treatment, including savage personal attacks.

You get the picture. Each mountain requires some skills and character, but these can be acquired and developed by anyone who is called to any particular mountain. All that you really need is the determination to fulfill your destiny and the rest will follow.

Complacency – A Major Enemy

Complacency occurs when we get used to situations and conditions over which we feel we have little power, but complacency perpetuates those situations and prevents us from bringing change.

Webster's dictionary on the internet defines complacency this way:

> *Self-satisfaction, especially when accompanied by unawareness of actual dangers or deficiencies.*

God's people have certainly been unaware of "actual dangers or deficiencies" that happen to our society when wicked men and women rule the seven mountains of society. And in many ways, we have been self-satisfied with our position in society, unaware that we could actually make a difference on one of these mountains.

The purpose of this chapter is to stir your heart and mind to shake off complacency and come to a realization that God wants to recruit you to be a king on a mountain. So let's take a brief look at where our society stands in regard to each of the seven mountains.

Don't Get Discouraged

Before you get too overwhelmed with what we are about to share, I want to give you the good news. We are making progress and God is raising up many leaders who are mobilizing a great army to conquer the seven mountains of society. So as you read the following pages, be aware that God has given us a plan and that plan is being put into play.

I. THE FAMILY MOUNTAIN

Compared to education, entertainment, government, business and media, the family mountain doesn't seem to be as powerful or influential a mountain on the surface. But think of this: Your body is made up of cells that seem individually insignificant, but the health of the cells determines the health of your body. Even so the health of a society depends on the health of the families in that society.

The average family in our western society is extremely unhealthy and severely lacking in basic family nutrition. We have been feeding on junk food for too long and our family systems are breaking down, in the same way that your immune system, your cardiovascular system and your digestive system begin to break down when your body is starved for proper nutrition.

The result of the failure of the family is impacting society in every way. The majority of the problems we face in society on every mountain result directly from the lack of character and emotional stability that should come from a healthy family. Crime and poverty are usually just symptoms of sick families, or the lack of the fruit of healthy families.

Statistics vary from one survey to another, but we know that traditional marriage has been under attack in many ways. More children live without both natural parents than ever before. Divorce may be declining some, but it is only because fewer people bother to get married. Teen pregnancies, abortions, sexually transmitted diseases and domestic violence are some of the symptoms of the crisis on the family mountain.

We can't get into all the reasons for the breakdown of the family, but we can say that it has been a key strategy of the enemy of our souls for a long, long time, and he has succeeded far more than we are even aware. He has used a lot of different tactics to accomplish this, including dominating the arts and entertainment mountain and the education mountain.

At this point, we need to focus on the solution, which is replacing ungodly kings on the family mountain. At the same, the kings on the other mountains that have such a profound influence on the family mountain need to be replaced. We need to look at the various positions available on the family mountain and begin to ask God if He wants us to take dominion somewhere on that mountain. Then we need to ask Him for the wisdom to make war in a godly way with those who want to perpetuate the dissolution and destruction of the family.

How can we replace the junk food diet with healthy nutrition that will restore the family's health? How can we convince the family to change their diet, when junk food is much more convenient and also seems to taste a lot better? These are questions that require God's supernatural wisdom to answer, but He will give us that wisdom if we ask Him.

Positions Available on the Family Mountain

1. Kingdom-minded Parents

Before we spend too much time trying to fix society's problems on the family mountain, we should make every effort to establish our own family as a kingdom-minded force for good. People are searching for examples and models to imitate. I know teenagers who have told me they aren't sure they want to get married and have a family, because they haven't seen any families that look like they are happy.

Most families today have so much stress that the husband and wife are constantly at war with each other. Complicate that with independent-minded teenagers fighting for their rights and privileges and you have a pretty ugly picture. Recently, we were prophesying to some older couples and the Lord spoke to them that their amazing loving relationship had brought hope to so many younger people who were struggling with their own relationships. Just having one or two examples to look up to gives people hope that they can have a happy life themselves.

With all of the enemy's lethal weapons aimed at the family today, it takes strong determination, commitment and God's amazing grace to make a marriage and family succeed, but God has provided many excellent tools for this generation and it is not impossible or too hard for God. To get started in improving your own marriage, you can start with what we discussed in chapter one.

It will take a good dose of humility for both partners to enjoy a loving relationship, but the rewards of humility are both huge and wonderful according to the Word of God. First of all, God gives grace to the humble (James 4:6), and we need God's grace every day. Secondly, God promises to exalt the humble (Matthew 23:12). This is how we gain position on any mountain.

The hardest place to practice humility is in our home, but it is where we demonstrate and expose the feelings and motives of our heart. We must all let God use our spouse, children, parents and other family members to expose our ugly flesh and deal with it by putting the ax to the root and stopping the growth of the poisonous fruit. From a polluted root comes poisonous fruit.

2. Kingdom-minded Family Counselors

When you have learned some key lessons for a Kingdom family, you can be a resource for others who are still struggling in areas you have found victory. You can share your insights with young people and young couples and even older couples. You can start one-on-one, but the time may come for you to teach classes, seminars and conferences.

You might want to take professional training and become an expert in marriage and family counseling. You might write articles or books to assist others who would like to learn what you have already discovered. As you can see there are many positions available on this part of the family mountain.

3. Kingdom-minded Family Advocates or Activists

When it comes to the efforts to change the definition of marriage or family, or the definition and value of life, many people can have a place on the mountain to bring positive change and stop the negative progress of the enemy. Obviously, we need to challenge those who presently have great impact, who are little-by-little restructuring our values that relate to life and family.

Again, there are many positions on this part of the mountain. You might start small by stirring up a few friends and family in church or at your job. Going to the next level would be a grass-roots movement, which could grow to a much larger place of impact and transformation.

PERSONAL CHECKUP TIME #4

1. How much has society's complacency affected you and others around you?

2. Do you have other families or couples that you look up to as role models?

3. Do you see your own marriage or family as a role model for others?

4. Have you discovered the power of humility to resolve family conflicts?

5. Are you ever involved in counseling others in their family conflicts?

6. Have you been involved in family values activism?

II. THE RELIGION MOUNTAIN

Understanding who sits on the throne of this mountain is probably more difficult than all of the other mountains. Certainly, this mountain has been divided up into many sections, but who is really at the top? Who wields the most influence from this mountain and what is our challenge when it comes to possessing it for the Kingdom of Heaven?

From the world's perspective, this mountain is pretty much insignificant and irrelevant. The Roman Catholic Church still has a lot of people looking to it for guidance although a large number of them won't agree with some of its basic doctrines such as the sanctity of life. Other traditional denominations such as Lutherans, Presbyterians, Methodists and Episcopalians also get some public attention, but their influence for bringing Heaven's Kingdom to earth is rather minimal.

Fundamentalists and evangelicals, including the many brands of Baptists, have some influence, but they are also considered somewhat eccentric and mocked by a large portion of the general public. These groups have regional strongholds, especially in the American southern states, and they work hard to bring the truth of salvation to as many people as possible. Unfortunately, most of them are cessationists, not believing that God is still doing miracles and imparting supernatural gifts of the Holy Spirit to the church. The result is that they don't have the impact that they could.

Pentecostals and Charismatics believe in the supernatural power of God, but like other movements, most of them have not maintained their zeal and passionate love for God that they started with. Many divisions have occurred which has helped to stall their forward progress. Instead of working together, they have often competed for position with each other. In addition, because of the way the world has seen them on television and other media, they have been treated with disdain. The general public looks at them as phonies who, like the classic snake oil salesmen, are just trying to get their money.

Many other sub-groups exist and have impact in various ways. The prophetic and apostolic movement has begun to permeate most religious groups with an understanding of a new way of thinking about church and the Kingdom of Heaven on the earth. Although these groups are still small, they have some interaction with other mountains of society, but their overall influence is not yet bringing about significant change in the church at large or the world.

In addition, there are some strong religious groups like Jehovah's Witnesses, Mormons and Christian Scientists. They also have staked their claims on the Religion Mountain. Jehovah's Witnesses and Mormons, in particular, have pushed their influence with aggressive recruiting practices.

Many non-Christian religions are also staking their claims on the religion mountain in the western world and demanding equal rights. Eastern religions have influenced our society for many decades. New Age teachings have attracted multitudes with their flavor of the supernatural, which appeals to many. But what may be causing the most concern today is the rapid increase and spread of Islam. Muslims are taught basic kingdom principles of multiplication and dominion. While Europeans and those of European descent average less than two children per couple, Muslims average eight children per couple. They believe they will end up controlling America and the world, and they are infiltrating every segment of society today. They understand the importance of taking over the seven mountains better than the church today.

Today the very concept of the equality of all religions, a perverted view of what America's founding fathers believed, is threatening the complete overthrow of basic Christianity on the Religion Mountain.

Importance of Who Controls the Religion Mountain

We might tend to underestimate the value of controlling this mountain. Our Kingdom is not of this world and we are converting hearts, not public opinion. But it is very important to our future that when people don't know where else to look for help, they know they can look to Christians and the church of Jesus Christ.

When the 9-11 tragedy occurred, people flocked to churches. They hoped to find answers and help. Some did, but most never came back. Today, probably less people attend church than before 9-11. If we share the top of this mountain with hundreds of other religions, people will look less and less to Jesus as their answer, trying every other alternative. We need to be there when they need us and they need to know that it is Jesus, not Buddha or Mohammed, who can help them.

I believe our goal as the people of God should be to take this mountain for the Kingdom of God. I believe that we will know that this mountain really belongs to God when the Media and Entertainment Mountains begin to portray God and His people in a positive light and when the government mountain changes laws to stop restricting the freedom of Christian activities in public places.

Positions Available on the Religion Mountain

Five-fold Ministries

Apostles, prophets, evangelists, pastors and teachers all have very important positions to fill on the Religion Mountain. But being a Kingdom-minded servant-minister with a five-fold ministry gift is different than just having a gift and using it to build your ministry. The anointing brings a following, but only those who truly put first His Kingdom can fulfill His purpose for their lives and truly represent Him on the earth.

Those who serve the King of Kings and His subjects with a humble heart will be given a more prominent place on the religion mountain. I personally believe every Christian can find fulfillment in one or more of these callings, starting at an apprentice level, like the young apostle, Timothy, and maturing to a higher calling, like the Apostle Paul. Faithfulness with humility equals great promotion. The King of Kings has larger thrones in higher places available, and He is waiting for someone to qualify for a promotion from Him.

Apostles can be found on every mountain of society, but on the religion mountain they are called to use God's wisdom to strategize the takeover of more territory for the Kingdom of Heaven. They administrate and facilitate growth. They plan their offense and their defense well, seeing the big picture and knowing the tactics of their enemy. Along with the prophets, they empower all the other ministries.

Prophets reveal the heart of the Father and the mind of Christ. They edify, exhort and comfort the people of God with updates from the King of Kings. Prophets prepare the way for others, especially those with miracle ministries, as John the Baptist prepared the way for Jesus. Prophets spend time learning to listen and discern the voice of God so they can be a true blessing to His people.

Evangelists bring good news of salvation, healing and deliverance and are in short supply in the church today and certainly in need of a better public image. Most people in the world think of televangelists when they hear the word "evangelist" and their opinions are less than favorable. People think evangelists are only in it for the money and fame, and see them as being less trustworthy than a used car salesman. But true evangelists need to be empowered by the apostles and prophets and supported financially, because they are the ones who really expand the Kingdom of Heaven on earth. When they don't need to raise their own support, they will not be as inclined to manipulate people for their own survival.

Pastors are people who care for the sheep and the lambs. They bring healing, love and encouragement. Not all church leaders are pastors by gifting. Many are really apostles, some are prophets or evangelists and some are teachers.

Calling them all pastors has created problems, since a title presumes a job description. Instead of fulfilling their God-given callings, they try to be caretakers of the sheep, when they should be doing other things for which God has gifted them. Our present church structure, however, does not provide any ministry income if they don't take some position with the title of "pastor". So to stay in ministry, they try to fulfill the desires of the sheep in the barn, rather than go get more sheep as an evangelist, or research truth to teach, as a teacher, or spend time seeking the face of God for His fresh word, as a prophet, etc.

Teachers can bring great transformation and freedom to the church by releasing fresh truth and revelation. Truth brings freedom and fresh ideas and can change the way people act. Teachers can have a profound impact on the church and the world. People who have had teachers who have taught them that God does not do miracles anymore, seldom see anything supernatural because they don't believe in miracles and they don't ask for them. But when uneducated people in Africa are taught that God still does miracles, they heal the sick and raise the dead. Teachers are needed at all levels, from the very young to church leaders.

Top Level Leaders at the Top of the Mountain

The truth is that the church of Jesus Christ could use a multitude of Kingdom-minded leaders at every level, but I believe there is a special need for true spiritual leaders at the top of this mountain. Of course, the Roman Catholics have a pope, whom they look up to, and every denomination has a president or top leader, but to whom does main-stream America look up to for spiritual guidance today?

In recent decades, there was no doubt about whom people respected and trusted the most for spiritual leadership. It was Billy Graham by a mile. Today the Koreans have David Yongi Cho and Africa has Reinhardt Bonke, but there is no one in America or any other western nation who has stepped in to fill the vacuum left by the retirement of Billy Graham from public ministry in his late eighties. There are many leaders near the top, but no one with the respect and admiration of the majority of Americans.

I believe the question is: Whom can God trust with so much honor and influence that they will be able to rule from the top of the mountain without falling into the temptations of pride, arrogance, greed and/ or moral failure, as so many others have in the past? Almost everyone would acknowledge that Billy Graham was able to accomplish that, and God gave him incredible honor and favor with presidents and kings. In my heart, I would like to believe that God will raise up someone who believes in and practices the love of God, as well as the power of God with miracles, signs and wonders, and yet has a pure and humble heart and lives to serve others rather than to be served.

On the other hand, that glorious position on top of the Religion Mountain may be given not to one famous individual, but to a new generation of passionate lovers of Jesus who have accepted the role of those who fast and pray, worship and intercede for others. It has been prophesied that this nameless/faceless generation will fill stadiums and be on every news network, healing the sick and raising the dead and attracting the eyes of the world. They don't look for fame or fortune, just the presence and glory of God to which they have become addicted.

In whatever way God wants to rule this mountain, we know there is a lack of strong leadership at the top, no one is really in control and most of the world could not care less. It's time to rise up and make our move for the Kingdom of God. The world needs to know where to look in the times of crisis and your neighbor does, too. They need to see a light in the darkness that shines far brighter than the light of any other false religion.

PERSONAL CHECKUP TIME #5

1. Do you know which of the five ministries you are most inclined to?

2. Do you have a second ministry which is also strong?

3. How can you use this gifting in practical ways in church or para-church ministries?

4. Who controls the Religion Mountain in your region?

III. THE EDUCATION MOUNTAIN

Who can overestimate the importance of the Mountain of Education? Both Hitler and the Communist leaders knew the power of educating the children to believe like them. Islamic rulers also know it well. The current kings on top of the education mountain have believed in that power for some time. They themselves were taught by teachers who molded their minds to think a certain way. They have inherited their thrones from a long tradition of secular humanists that began their ascent approximately two centuries ago.

Horace Mann

Horace Mann is known as "The Father of American Education" because he pushed the concept of public schools for all. Before that, virtually all education was private. Most schools were church schools or home schools. Mann believed that educating everyone for free would eliminate all kinds of society's problems, including poverty. He believed education was the great answer to everything and he became the country's first Secretary of Education in 1837. He actually began some of the first public schools in America. His beliefs in science and education and rejection of religion were picked up by John Dewey and others in the twentieth century.

John Dewey

In 1933, several leaders, including philosopher John Dewey, came together to write the first Humanist Manifesto. It has been through two revisions since then. The basic idea was that we needed a new religion, based on science to replace what they called "superstitious religion", which was based on supernatural revelation. The new religion was called "Religious Humanism".

John Dewey began a forty-seven year career with New York City's Columbia University in 1904. It was the premier university for educating teachers. As a professor and prolific author, Dewey changed the way teachers thought and taught. His influence was enormous. As one of the chief signers of the first Humanist Manifesto, he gave it much recognition because of his great notoriety.

Humanist Manifesto II

In 1973, the Humanist Manifesto II was formulated. It included some radical statements that we need to read and understand. Here are some quotes:

"No deity will save us, we must save ourselves."

"The battle for humankind's future must be waged and won in the public school classroom by teachers who correctly perceive their role as the proselytizers of a new faith: a religion of humanity that recognizes and respects the spark of what theologians call divinity in every human being."

". . . utilizing a classroom instead of a pulpit to convey humanist values in whatever subject they teach, regardless of the educational level – preschool day care or large state university."

Obviously, humanists – atheists with a supposed concern for humanity – determined to use the mountain of education to replace all other religions of the western world and the USA in particular. The classroom was their pulpit and teachers were proselytizers of their faith – from preschool through university.

In 2003, a new revision of the Humanist Manifesto was released. This document reaffirmed the belief in empirical science, including the theory of evolution. Although we don't hear the term humanism as much anymore, the basic tenets of its faith are fully integrated within our entire education system. The humanists have almost totally succeeded in taking possession of the education mountain, leaving the church of Jesus Christ in the dust at the base of the mountain, wondering why things are going so badly in our education system.

The Mountainous Challenge

How do we conquer such a strong enemy that has such a stranglehold on the very top of this mountain? With many radical extremists, such as William Ayers and Ward Churchill, holding professorships with tenure in many universities and teaching colleges, the challenge is almost overwhelming, but the need is extremely desperate. These misguided pedagogues are perverting the minds and hearts of some of our brightest young people, robbing them of their eternal destiny. It's our innocent children who suffer from this demonic tyranny. We as God-fearing Christians, bring them into the world and turn them over to atheists who pervert their minds. Remember, God says "The fool has said in his heart, 'There is no God'" (Psalm 53:1). When atheists teach our children, they are being taught by fools. We must find a way to take this mountain back.

In some cases, we will utilize help from other mountains, such as government, business and religion. We need laws changed to restore the right to pray and discuss the Bible. We need finances to win court cases against the ACLU. We need intercessors to do spiritual warfare and evangelists to win the hearts and minds of those who are already teachers.

But much of the change will come from the bottom up and there is no time to waste. We need some of our brightest young people to work their way up this mountain. We also need existing Christian teachers and professors to ask God for a promotion to a place of higher influence. Recently, I shared some of these truths at a large church in South Korea. Before we left, a university professor came to us and promised that he would ask God to help him get promoted to a higher position, so he could have more influence on the education mountain.

Fields Related to Education

We would include science and technology as well as medicine on this mountain. They fit here better than on the other mountains because they are based on discovering and disseminating information. Of course, there is an overlap with the mountain of business and finance, but if you are involved in research or discovery, you can stake a claim to a kingdom on this mountain.

PERSONAL CHECKUP TIME #6

1. Do you feel called to the Education Mountain?

2. Do you know others who are serving on this mountain?

3. How can you support them and encourage them to go higher?

4. Who controls the education mountain in your local schools and colleges?

5. Have you checked out the school's text books for what's in them and what's left out?

6. Have you ever gone to a school board meeting to stand up for what's right?

7. Do you have a scientific mind? Does the field of medicine appeal to you?

IV. THE GOVERNMENT MOUNTAIN

I am particularly passionate about this mountain. This mountain has so much power to do good or evil, and we have been on such a teeter-totter for so long. Sometimes the forces of justice get stronger, but before long it seems the forces of injustice push back what little gains we have made. Overall, it seems clear to me that the enemy has had much more control of this mountain than the people of the Kingdom in the past century or so.

Many Christians think they are doing their duty by getting out to vote every four years or so. But we need to look at the political process, not as a duty, but as a God-given opportunity to impact our community, the nation and the world. There are so many different thrones to occupy on this mountain. From local school boards to city counsels to mayors, to state or provincial representatives, senators and governors or premiers, to federal representatives, senators, judges, advisors, cabinet secretaries, and president or prime minister, you have a lot of choices and a lot of opportunities.

Running for political office can be a very difficult job and the opposition to a Christian can be incredible, as Governor Sarah Palin of Alaska recently discovered. But there are great rewards, and there are amazing opportunities to accomplish great things for the Kingdom of Heaven on the earth.

The 2008 USA elections showed us what happens when the leaders on the religion mountain cannot get their acts together and work in unity. Almost every top Christian leader chose to support a different candidate. But I believe God is up to something and will not forsake America, even though America has largely forsaken God. God has a plan to use America in the great harvest, which is now upon us, and He will do miraculous things to bring America back to God. This will include putting His choice – a David, rather than a Saul – in the White House.

One reason for hope is that God loves to restore broken covenants when His people return to Him. The Mayflower Compact, signed by the Pilgrims, was declared by them to be a covenant among brothers in the sight of God. The Pilgrims came for one main purpose, which was to practice their Christian faith in freedom. I believe God has not forgotten the passion and commitment of our founding fathers, even as He remembers His covenants with Abraham, Isaac and Jacob, not to mention David and Solomon.

Getting Started

If God has given you some passion for politics, like He has given me, you can do many things, including running for office. But you can first get involved in the campaigns of other charactered Christian leaders. You can pray and intercede and inform people of the issues at stake. You can donate and help raise funds. In today's world, you can't win an election without some resources.

One thing that bothers me about many Christians in America is that they wait until the big elections to vote. It's in the primaries that we usually have some decent choices, and it's easier to make a difference because fewer people come out to vote. If the majority of Christians got together to support the best candidate for president in the primaries first and then the general election, they could probably get that person elected.

If you want to run for office to bring the Kingdom change needed, you need to study and research the position you desire and find out who is willing to support you from the start. If God says, "Do it!" then do it, but also use all the wisdom God has given you. You need the confidence and authority that only comes from Heaven, but you need to also maintain a humble heart and be willing to admit mistakes and apologize quickly when you've made one.

You need to expose the policies of anti-Kingdom politicians without attacking them personally. You need to explain why their policies are not good for the people they represent. You also need to ask God for creative ideas and the spirit of revelation that Daniel and Joseph had.

You will also need special wisdom when you get attacked for being "religious". You shouldn't use your faith to promote yourself, but you also should not be ashamed of your faith or apologize for it. You can simply state that you love God and your country and believe in the Golden Rule, integrity, honesty, justice and compassion.

If you don't win your first election, don't quit. You will learn a lot from a defeat and you don't want to waste all that good knowledge. Try again and let your name become familiar with the voters. Love people and they will love you.

When you do win your first election, do everything you can to serve the people with honesty and integrity. At the same time as God opens the doors, use your experience as a stepping stone to a higher place on the mountain, not for personal ambition, like most politicians, but for influence and impact for the Kingdom. Learn to be wise as a serpent and harmless as a dove. Keep your record as pure and clean as possible without the appearance of compromise and stay humble. There are great doors of opportunity a little higher up the mountain, and God is looking for those He can trust to fill those positions.

PERSONAL CHECKUP TIME #7

1. Have you ever run for office of any kind, including at school?

2. Have you ever helped as a campaign volunteer?

3. Have you gone to prayer and repentance rallies such as The Call D.C. to pray for the elections?

4. Do you have the right personality and gifting for public office?

5. What talents and gifts would make for a good Christian politician?

V. THE MEDIA AND COMMUNICATION MOUNTAIN

This mountain has a lot of overlap with the Arts and Entertainment Mountain, which we will look at next, but we are focusing on modern means of dispensing information, rather than entertaining the masses. We are dealing with television networks, radio and newspaper communication, along with the vast array of internet communication sites.

While we have some great Christian networks and stations, no one would say that Christians control or dominate this mountain. Our mainstream networks have been slanting the news against Kingdom values for many decades. We now have one major network, Fox News, which is more conservative than the others and comes from a mostly Roman Catholic perspective. However, the vast combined power of all the older networks has been very influential in helping to get liberal politicians elected. These networks also were involved in aggressive attacks on Sarah Palin, a family-values Christian vice-presidential candidate. At the same time they gave Senator Obama an almost free ride to the White House.

In any close election, getting the favor of the media can almost assure you of victory. News networks usually try to portray a non-biased image, but that is virtually impossible. There are many subtle, but powerful, ways to promote a certain agenda with news reporting. It's not just what stories they cover, but also what stories they do not cover. By ignoring certain events and activities, the majority of their listeners will never know that those events and activities are happening.

For instance, Christians have held huge gatherings of hundreds of thousands of people at Washington, DC to repent for America's sins. The news media barely covered the events at all, and if they do, they will grossly underestimate the number of people attending. But if six angry people protest against something we believe in, the cameras are all over the story. They will cover a gay parade, but not a march for life. If they cover a Right to Life Rally, they will focus mostly on the pro-abortion protesters.

If a tremendous revival is taking place with thousands of people attending night after night, the cameras won't show up until it's been going on for weeks or months. Any coverage will usually be with a tongue-in-cheek tone of voice, especially if there are claims of miracles happening. Special news programs like 60 Minutes may do programs investigating TV preachers like Benny Hinn. Their clear objective is to discredit the preachers. They had a field day with Jimmy Swaggart, Jim Bakker and Ted Haggard, who were all involved in sex or money scandals.

Basically, the masses in America and other western countries are kept in the dark about the most important events going on in the world. These news networks are owned by a handful of powerful non-Kingdom-minded people and they control and/or influence the content of news in their chains.

Because of the internet and the free and easy access to news today, newspaper dynasties are crumbling. Many are going out of business or offering their news only on the internet. This gives the internet an even more prominent place in the dispensing of information.

The internet is a tremendous opportunity for common people, including Kingdom-minded Christians, to have an influence and impact. There are some strong Christians who have made an impact with various internet companies, but there is an open door right now for many more Kingdom-minded saints to stake their claim on this mountain of media.

Getting Involved in the Media Mountain

Some years ago, I worked for a small newspaper. At first I just worked in the print shop, but after writing numerous letters to the editor on subjects such as politics and education, they asked me to fill in for the sports writer they had just fired. This position opened many doors of opportunity for me. I could interview students and coaches and other school officials. In addition, it gave me some visibility and impact in a small town. When I wrote positive reports about the student athletes, it opened the hearts of the parents, as well as the athletes.

One of the easiest ways to get involved in media is to write letters to the editor and see if they will get published. Even easier than that, you can write comments on the internet, responding to news stories, etc. You can also use websites like facebook.com, utube.com, myspace.com or twitter.com to communicate your thoughts and views. If you enjoy writing in these media, you might enjoy taking it to a higher level.

If you feel God's call to this mountain, you may want to make a more serious study of journalism, or find a job working for a radio or TV station. When you work around a media business, you will be confronted with other opportunities for advancement. Pray for God to give you favor for His glory. Don't be complacent with just a "good job". Ask God to give you a throne on the mountain that will have great impact and influence for the King of Kings and His wonderful Kingdom.

Many people from the Religion Mountain have been on Christian television or radio. It's possible to have some influence and impact in these media, but these ministries, like most church ministries, mainly reach other Christians and have little influence on non-Christians in a secular world. It's time for those with callings on this mountain to pursue a spirit of excellence and integrity in the challenging world of the media and communication mountain.

PERSONAL CHECKUP TIME #8

1. Have you witnessed media bias when it comes to religion or politics?

2. Have you ever written a letter to the editor or a commentary on the internet?

3. Have you ever spoken on a radio or TV program?

4. Are you good with audio or visual recording or other related technology?

5. Do you know anyone working on this mountain that you can encourage to go to a higher level?

VI. THE ARTS AND ENTERTAINMENT MOUNTAIN

This particular mountain of our society has more influence and impact today than at any time in the history of the western world. From Hollywood, Broadway, Nashville and many other locations, movies and music are being churned out at a rapid pace which a generation of hurting and bored people are consuming and devouring. More people today get their information about the world from arts and entertainment than from news networks. The younger generation, especially, finds more time for television comedies, movies and music than they do for education or work.

Arts, of course, includes music, drama, dance, writing, painting, sketching, photography and various variations and combinations of the above, along with the producing and directing of movies and other dramatic performances. All of the above varieties of the arts, along with any that I might have missed, offer incredible opportunities for Kingdom-minded Christians for powerful impact on the world.

Our five children have all participated on this mountain and it has been quite exciting for each of them. Our daughter, Andrea, a graduate of Christ for the Nations in Dallas, Texas, was privileged to travel to several overseas nations using drama, mime and human video to present the gospel, under the ministry of Kaleidoscope, directed by Rayanna Fields. She also spent time teaching and training others, both in Christian high schools and in overseas college-level ministry.

This mountain appeals to the younger generation far more than any other, and it is one of the greatest opportunities for Kingdom invasion today. The American Idol program, a singing contest on American TV, attracts incredible attention, and a number of Christian worship leaders and soloists have entered the contest and done extremely well. Those who win the competition can then use their incredible platform to share the love of God with their performances and the CD's that millions will buy. This is just one of today's opportunities on the Arts and Entertainment Mountain.

God has also been moving on numerous saints to produce inspired and prophetic painting and photography. Our friend, Robert Bartow, has produced some amazing works through his camera and computer. His pictures have graced the covers of many books, including most of mine. Christian dance teams have also multiplied and have gone to new levels of skill and anointing. We are very excited by the progress made on this mountain and look forward to a greater explosion in the future.

Book writing also falls into the Arts and Entertainment category, and is still a great way to make an impact on the world. After I had written several books, I was asked to teach part of a seminar on book writing. From those notes I responded to the requests of others and wrote a book entitled, *Birthing the Book Within You*. Of course, I highly recommend it for all who feel called to write.

Another huge field on the entertainment side of the mountain is sports. Millions of people watch sporting events every day, and those who have a prominent place on this part of the mountain can use their platform for the Kingdom of Heaven on earth. God does call some of His kids to use their God-given talents in sports for His glory.

PERSONAL CHECKUP TIME #9

1. Do you minister in music, or have you done so in the past?

2. Have you ever done any acting?

3. Was it something you enjoyed or felt good at?

4. Are you gifted in painting, sketching or photography?

5. Do you have other talents like dance or creating things with your hands?

6. Have you ever felt you were called to write a book?

7. Do you know anyone, young or old who is especially gifted on this mountain that you could encourage or support on their way to a higher place?

VII. THE MOUNTAIN OF BUSINESS AND FINANCE

Like no other mountain, this mountain impacts every other mountain. Every family, church, school, political entity, media outlet and arts project needs a flow of finances to survive and prosper. The higher anyone gets on this mountain, the more power and influence he or she has on all the others.

Today, the world of business and finance is controlled by not only non-believers, but by a small group of incredibly wealthy international bankers with names such as Rothschild, Rockefeller, Kennedy, Morgan, etc., who have an agenda to bring the whole world under their control. They influence the world's economies, help start and finance wars and ultimately bring governments into slavery through debt.

This mountain is one of the least inhabited by Kingdom-minded saints. For Christians, it is probably one of the most dangerous mountains to conquer for a couple of reasons.

First of all, this is the most cut-throat territory on the earth. Men will do almost anything to go to a higher position and keep it on this mountain. Trying to unseat someone from their throne on this mountain will bring a major counterattack. For someone who has had the benefits of wealth, it is devastating to have to give those benefits up.

Many people who lost their fortunes in the Great Depression committed suicide, not because they were starving, but because they couldn't face living without wealth. This has also happened in recent times when the Bernie Madoff scandal was made public and people realized they had lost tens of millions of dollars. The same has happened to many who have gambled away their wealth. I once talked with a reporter being hired in Nevada, who mentioned that the newspapers never report on suicides in Las Vegas, because it would be bad for the gambling business, and the Casinos would boycott the newspapers, causing them to go out of business.

Secondly, the mountain of finance is dangerous for Christians because of the difficulty us mortals have to stay humble when we have wealth and the power that comes with it. Jesus commented on how hard it was for a rich man to enter Heaven. Without the grace of God received through continuous humbling, we could not pass this test. However, without Kingdom-minded saints on this mountain, we cannot facilitate the harvest and the work of God on all of the other mountains.

I know that in this hour of history, God's eyes are searching throughout the whole earth to find people with the humble and sold-out hearts that He can trust to rule on this very important mountain. There are many positions on this mountain, and there are many Christians occupying some of the lower places on the mountain. But God wants to promote them to a higher place where they can begin to have influence and impact on this mountain itself, as well as all the other mountains of society.

PERSONAL CHECKUP #10

1. Do you have strong desires to own your own business?

2. Do you have special wisdom or strategy for investing or saving?

3. Do you try to support good Christian businesses?

4. Do you feel the burden of people who need financial help?

5. Are you an inventor at heart?

6. Do you know wise people in business who could mentor you?

This has been a long chapter, yet we have only scratched the surface when it comes to the seven mountains of society. There is much more that could be said about each of them, but our purpose is to convince every reader that there are tremendous needs on these mountains, and

God is looking for people who are willing to take the pressure and stand strong as kings representing the King of Kings.

We want now to focus our attention on how you can know with more certainty what mountain or mountains you belong on. Where should you focus your energy, and how should you plan your future? I believe you will find it very helpful to you and those you teach these principles.

CHAPTER FOUR

HOW DO I KNOW WHERE I BELONG?

Many people already know where they belong, but there are a lot of others who are quite confused as to which mountain they should climb for God. Some will have inclinations and desires for ruling in two or three mountains and this might be part of the confusion. I believe for practical purposes, we should try to prioritize our mountains and attempt to focus on which one has the strongest attraction. We can have a major and a minor or two, like we would in college or university. The following insights should help you put your mountains in order until God reveals any adjustments and changes He desires to make in your life.

I. DESIRES AND DREAMS

The first clue to the right mountain for you will come from your own heart. God promised to give us the desires of our heart if we delight ourselves in Him. That Scripture can be interpreted two ways, but I believe both interpretations apply. The first interpretation is that He, Himself, puts the right desires in our hearts when we delight in Him. The second is that He really does give us the things that are hearts desire, as long as they are wholesome desires.

Dreams are very closely related to desires, but they can come in several forms. The first is the literal dream you have when you are sleeping. These dreams may come from your subconscious mind and relate to your desires.

On the other hand, these dreams could be what we would call "God-dreams", or dreams in which God comes and shows you things He wants to reveal to you. Dreams are usually symbolic and in need of interpretation. The Bible is full of stories of God speaking to people in dreams. The most famous in the Old Testament are Joseph's dreams, Pharaoh's dreams, Nebuchadnezzar's dreams, and Daniel's dreams. In the New Testament we have the Wise Men's dreams and Joseph's dreams. Others had night visions. Many times angels spoke in the dreams as a more direct message from God.

Most of our God-dreams are not as clear as those mentioned above. Many of them are difficult to understand and may require someone with special gifting or training to interpret them.

Another type of dream is what we usually call a day-dream. These can be from God, as much as a night-dream. You can yield your mind to the Holy Spirit and ask Him to direct your subconscious thoughts and amplify them to the level that they become part of your conscious thinking. These day-dreams usually involve some kind of a wish, such as, "Wouldn't it be awesome if we could afford to support that orphanage so they could take another hundred kids." Or, "Some day we are going to open a Christian Coffee Shop."

You probably had some exciting dreams when you were very young. I remember watching some great revival preachers and thinking to myself, "That's what I want to do." We lived in a community without running water in the early 1950's and had an outhouse in the back yard. I remember preaching to an imaginary congregation in that little outhouse. It was the only place where I could be alone. We lived in a small house and I had three siblings.

Perhaps you work where you do just because you need a job and you took what was available. But your dreams were far different than your life right now. If you sense that your dreams came from Heaven, it's time to stir those dreams up again. God can fulfill your dream, but you may be required to give up your comfort zone and security to move to the mountain God has prepared for you.

I'm not encouraging people to leave their jobs without divine confirmation and wise counsel, but I'm also not in favor of people staying in bondage to an unfulfilling job when they have a passion to do something for God on another mountain. God will provide where He will guide, but we need to know that we have heard the voice of God.

II. PROPHETIC ENCOURAGEMENT

Almost everyone has received prophetic words from someone, even if they don't believe in them. It may be a loving aunt or uncle, parent or grandparent, teacher or friend, who says just the right thing at the right time. God often works through unbelievers, and if He wants to speak to you, He can usually find someone to speak for Him.

For instance, a teacher might say, "You are really good with words. You'd make a good public speaker." Or, "You could become a good writer with your imagination." If something inside you leaped for joy when you heard a word like that, it could very well be an encouraging word from the Lord.

Most of my readers, however, have had clear prophetic words from a variety of prophetic people. Many have tapes, some of which have been transcribed onto paper for easy access. Some of you have been picked out of a crowd and given a word from God.

Any of these words which resonate in your spirit probably reveal some strong clues as to which mountain you belong on. A friend of mine was told he would become a "great and mighty giver", which confirmed to him that he belonged on the business and finance mountain. I was told in my youth by prophets that I would have certain spiritual gifts and ministries, confirming that I was called to the Religion Mountain.

My advice to everyone who has received such words and has a record of them is to read or listen to them with this specific question in mind:

"Are they indicating any particular mountain in their words to me?" If you see a consistent pattern, it probably indicates where you belong. Of course, your own spirit should confirm that conclusion.

III. RECOGNIZE YOUR PASSIONS AND BURDENS

What stirs your emotions? When you find yourself being touched in a special way by the presence of God, do you feel His heart of compassion for any segment of society? Do you sense that He is grieved with something going on in the world you live in?

What in society makes you angry? What makes you want to change your world? Is it local, regional, national or international politics? Or is it church politics? Perhaps it's child abuse, racial prejudice, human trafficking, pornography, poverty or illiteracy.

When something burdens you or fills you with righteous anger, there's a good chance God wants to raise you up to do something about it. Do you gravitate to other people with the same passions? That is another good sign you have a place with your name on it on one of society's mountains.

IV. REVIEW THE PATH YOUR LIFE HAS TAKEN

If you look back on your life and examine the path it has taken, you might also discover some clues to your destiny. Based on the belief that the steps of a good man are ordered by the Lord, we should be able to see the guiding hand of God preparing us for our destiny on the past journey of our life.

What clear divine appointments have you had with people you would never have expected to meet? What information have you become exposed to? Who do you connect with in the soul and spirit realm? What special classes have you been led to take? What skills and talents have you developed on your journey? Do these point to any particular mountain?

V. PUTTING IT ALL TOGETHER

Now take time to look at points 1 - 4 and see if there is any consistent pattern. What kind of desires and dreams have you carried with you over most of your life? What kind of prophetic words have come your way? What are your passions and burdens? And what kind of path has your journey been on?

Can you see a pattern? Can you visualize the next possible step to continue your journey and fulfill your destiny? Can you believe that God can use you and promote you in spite of your faults and weaknesses? If you can, there is nothing that can stop you from finding your place to rule and reign on the mountain of God's choosing for you.

Now, we must deal with an extremely important issue for all kings who are willing to accept the responsibility of ruling and reigning with God. It's the one great issue that will make or break us. How we deal with it will determine if we become a great asset to the King of kings or an embarrassment to Him. In the next chapter we must do the most important check-up in this book.

PERSONAL CHECKUP TIME #11

1. Who are your biggest heroes – people you would like to emulate?

2. Have you suppressed your desires and dreams or acknowledged them to be from God?

3. Are you afraid that if you go after your dreams you might fail and totally lose your dreams?

4. What personal accomplishments have brought you the most joy?

Chapter Five

How Do I Keep My Motives Pure?

As we discussed in *Kings and Kingdoms*, there are two ditches to fall into. On one side is the ditch of pride and selfish ambition. On the other side is false humility and complacency.

We all have the ability to have wrong or mixed motives in anything we do and we know that God looks not so much at our actions as the motives of our hearts. So how can we be sure we are not trying to become kings for our own personal honor and glory? Maybe we just love having power and authority over others because we are a bit insecure. Should we avoid taking a higher place on the mountain because we fear our motives are not perfect? Let me share a couple of special insights that will confirm you in your pursuit of that place on your mountain.

King Solomon

No earthly king could boast the grandeur and splendor of Solomon and his glorious kingdom. The Pharaohs of Egypt had made their mark in history, building pyramids and extending their domain beyond the region of the Nile River. After Solomon, many powerful and wealthy emperors ruled over most of the known world. But even those emperors could not equal the wealth and wisdom of King Solomon. Even before his reign, David had gathered and given him such a vast amount of gold and silver and other precious materials for the temple that his resources could easily have been worth more than a trillion dollars at today's values.

Most Christians know well the story of God visiting Solomon in a dream and giving him the opportunity to ask for anything he wanted. We all know that Solomon asked for wisdom and understanding rather than riches, glory and fame. We know that God was pleased with his request and gave him both what he had asked for and what he had not asked for. But there's something few have ever noticed in Solomon's petition to God. It may seem small, but I believe it is extremely important for all of us who would be kings under our King of kings.

After God spoke to Solomon and asked him for his heart's desire, Solomon humbly expressed his gratitude to God for allowing him to rule in the place of his father, David. Then he confessed to God how needy he was and declared himself to be just a child. Then he began to talk about the task that was before him and in the process he stated something three separate times in two verses (I Kings 3:8,9). What was that one thing he stated three times?

Stewardship vs. Ownership

Solomon simply stated that the people he was to rule over belonged to God. He used the expressions, "Your people" and "this great people of Yours". Solomon realized that God was the true King over all the people and all of his kingdom. God was his King of kings and Solomon, like us, was simply a steward of a portion of God's Kingdom. If we can just get that into our spirit and keep it there, the task of keeping our motives pure will be relatively easy.

The concept of stewardship as opposed to ownership is foundational to all of us who are willing to follow Jesus up the mountain. We may be shepherds leading other sheep, but we are also sheep following our Great Shepherd. We need to acknowledge our weakness and dependency on Him and not forget it as we move higher on our mountain.

A few years ago I had a vision during a conference worship session. I saw a majestic-looking Ram climbing the mountain of the Lord. He was looking back at the sheep which were following Him. I knew the ram represented the Lord. Later I remembered the ram caught in the thicket, which was the substitute sacrifice for Isaac. The ram was a type of Jesus, the Lamb of God.

Eye Contact

The Ram was looking to see who was focused on Him. He saw that many sheep were distracted with many things and were not keeping their eyes on Him. I heard Him saying, "I want eye contact with my sheep." If we keep our eyes on Him, He will guide us with His eye. (Psalm 32:8)

Looking into His loving eyes will keep us humble, yet confident, full of inner strength and determination. We are talking about intimacy with God. We are talking about a relationship that never takes a break with a God who never leaves us or forsakes us. We are talking about in all our ways acknowledging Him so that He can direct our paths. When we take our eyes off Him, they will be distracted by something else. King David discovered that the hard way.

For a short time in his reign over Israel, King David forgot that he was a steward, not an owner, of the kingdom. He took possession of someone else's wife and was rebuked by Nathan the prophet. Solomon also lost proper perspective later in life. If David could forget and if Solomon could forget, then we also must keep alert to the danger of becoming an owner rather than a steward of our kingdoms.

The Shepherd Psalm

A few years ago, I was blessed with a revelation concerning Psalm 23. I released that revelation in a book called, *With Me*. The truths found in that book relate in a wonderful way to the subject at hand. David, like few others, experienced the journey described in Psalm 23.

Yes, I now see Psalm 23 as the journey of any disciple of Jesus. You will find yourself somewhere on that journey today. Every step of that journey is important, but some may have been pushed too fast and not received the blessings available. Others may have gotten stuck and not progressed the way they should, staying babes when they should be teachers of others by now. Let's do a very quick "nutshell" version of the journey of Psalm 23.

The Baby Christian

It all began with the moment we realized that we needed a Shepherd and He entered our life. Immediately, He showed us where to find the gourmet grass and the sparkling water. Life was so exciting! We had never felt so loved and cared for and we were so excited about our Shepherd. Being a Christian was an amazing life.

Our human shepherds usually do a fair job of helping us at this first stage of our journey. The grass and water could represent the Word of God and the Holy Spirit.

Restoration of the Soul

In the next phase, our Good Shepherd restores our soul. This is where many have been pushed through to the next phase, without much help from their earthly shepherds, who, in an effort to make perfect disciples, try to lead them in paths of righteousness without fully restoring their soul. I certainly plead guilty (through ignorance) to missing this critical stage in the life of many of the sheep that I have had under my care in years past.

Today, we make restoring the soul a priority in the training of our team. Restoring the soul involves dealing with roots of bitterness and delivering people from past pain which produces undesirable behavior in their life. We shared some of these important things in the first chapter and encourage all readers to pursue more healing and restoration of the soul.

It's About Whom?

When the soul is restored a great transformation takes place which is the most critical event related to this subject. Our great Shepherd begins to lead us in paths of righteousness. The big change now is that there is a shift from everything being about us to everything being about Him. The key phrase now is, "FOR HIS NAME'S SAKE". As kings under our King of kings, everything must be for His name's sake, not for ours.

Paths of Righteousness

If we missed the soul restoration phase of the journey, this will be an extremely difficult part of the journey. An unhealed soul will respond badly when certain things take place during times of testing. The danger is that if this happens repeatedly, the wounded soul will want to give up and quit the journey, feeling that he or she is a total failure and incapable of pleasing God. The unhealed soul will not easily transition from the "It's about me!" stage to the "For His name's sake" stage. The soul, however, that is truly healed will find the journey not only bearable, but exciting and very fulfilling.

Intimacy in the Valley

As Jesus leads us in paths of righteousness, these paths take us through valleys, including the valley of the shadow of death. It is only His presence that keeps us from fear and in this place we learn a level of intimacy that we missed when gorging ourselves on gourmet grass and sparkling water. We become true disciples, following Him closely, learning from Him and serving Him in every way that we can. We gladly receive His correction and protection represented by His rod and staff.

Rewards of Intimacy

Finally, we emerge from the valley of testing, and He has prepared an amazing array of rewards and blessings. He honors us and feeds us at a beautiful banquet table, with our enemies watching. He pours on us His awesome anointing oil and then blesses us with every heavenly and earthly blessing. Through the intimacy and favor we have gained, we have perfect assurance that we will forever dwell in His presence in the House of the Lord.

These rewards are so very descriptive of the way Jesus makes us kings and priests on His mountain and the mountains of society. Those called to be kings under their King of kings will be given great honor. This honor will open doors of influence and impact and build a platform, not only for them, but also for others who can complement what they do.

These kings will also have a very strong anointing. This anointing will also open doors and bring great blessing to those they encounter and with whom they work. For instance, a healing anointing or a prophetic anointing will open doors into the hearts of unbelievers and even competitors. When God's miracle power is employed to meet the needs that no one else can, they will become friends and allies to the one who has blessed their life.

God's kings will also be blessed with incredible resources of Heaven and earth. Wealth can be a huge asset when you need to bring change to your mountain. God will transfer great wealth to His children on the mountains, and they will use it "for His name's sake.

Having a confidence and awareness of the fact that the King of Kings loves them and will provide a place for them throughout eternity will also remove all fear, including the fear of man. It will give these kings a powerful boldness to do great exploits, breaking tradition and violating political correctness.

God, Himself, has ordained and prepared a pathway for every king who will reign on the seven mountains. Each path is custom designed and will be what each person needs for his or her training for reigning.

PERSONAL CHECKUP TIME #12

1. How ambitious a person are you?

2. Have you felt jealous of other people in higher places on your mountain?

3. Have you felt a transition from "It's about me" to "For His name's sake"?

4. Have you developed intimacy in your valleys?

5. Has that intimacy helped you see yourself as a steward instead of an owner?

Chapter Six

Using Your Unfair Advantage

It's time to be reminded that God has given us some extremely high tech weapons to overthrow our enemy and conquer our mountains. These are the weapons against which there is no defense. We discussed them in some detail in Kings and Kingdoms, but let's now take a look at the expanded arsenal of the weapons of our warfare.

Before we look at the lists of spiritual gifts, let's look at some of the less obvious weapons God has given us. They truly give us an unfair advantage, which God has delighted in giving us.

Eternal Life

One great advantage that we have over anyone in the world is salvation or life that can't be taken away from us. In other words, we can be free from the handicap of fear of death or loss. Nothing of real value can be taken from us and we don't have to hold on to anything temporal because we have our treasures laid up in Heaven. The unbeliever only has the temporal and so he or she will be affected by the fear of death and loss. In Revelation 12:11, we are told that the saints overcame the enemy by not loving their own lives, even unto death.

The Blood of the Lamb and the Word of our Testimony

Of course, Revelation 12:11 also declares that they overcame the enemy by the blood of the Lamb and the word of their testimony as well. We are made righteous by His blood and our righteousness in His blood gives us favor with the Father, so we can effectively wage spiritual warfare and win. We also have the awesome power of our testimony, which unbelievers cannot compete with. As Bill Johnson of Bethel Church in Redding, California, likes to say, "A man with a theology or doctrine is no match for a man with an experience or testimony."

Prayer and Fasting, Worship and Praise

When the battle gets tough, true warrior-kings get down on their knees and take time to present their petitions and decrees to the King of kings. When they are not interceding they are in praise and worship mode. The presence of God is always with them. Favor and authority come from being in His presence and the enemy has no weapon or shield to defend against this authority.

Sacrificial Giving

Selfishness and greed prevail at the top of the seven mountains, and few unbelievers on those mountains know what to do with someone who, for no logical reason and nothing to gain, gives sacrificially of his or her time, energy and money to bless the unbelievers and their families. A man's gift makes room for him and sincere giving opens a multitude of doors.

The Heavenly Hosts – Legions of Angels

As children of our Heavenly Father, we can ask Him, as Jesus said He could, to send His angels to help us to do His will. More and more people are seeing these Heavenly beings and when they manifest their presence many amazing things happen. Some have seen angels standing at the side of preachers. When they whisper in the preacher's ear, a strong prophetic anointing falls on the preacher. When healing angels show up, incredible healing miracles take place. Angels of many kinds can help us climb to new heights on whatever mountain we serve.

We know that there are also demonic powers working against us – evil angels, if you will – but we know that our forces are more powerful than demons. Remember Moses' serpent devouring the Egyptian sorcerer's serpents. Remember, Elisha's servant's eyes being opened to see the hosts of Heaven surrounding the city.

Unity

Unity is a commodity with more potential than anyone really comprehends. It seems almost unachievable, but the early church possessed it and the results were extremely incredible. Jesus declared that when we, as His disciples, are working together in unity, the world will believe that God sent the Christ, His Son, into the world. When the people on our mountaintop become believers, the battle is over and we win the highest place of earthly influence. God will then use the body of Christ to bring the Kingdom of Heaven to earth as Jesus taught us to pray.

Spiritual Fruit

The impact of Holy Spirit empowered love is immeasurable. Nothing attracts people like true joy. And there is an amazing power in a life lived in the peace that passes all understanding. Longsuffering, kindness, goodness, faithfulness, gentleness and self-control are all divine high-tech weapons to defeat the enemy. Without using these, we will lose our unfair advantage, but with them working through the power of the Holy Spirit, we are more than conquerors.

Spiritual Gifts

When spiritual fruit and spiritual gifts are combined in a one-two punch, the results can be spectacular. The early Jerusalem church is an amazing example. Other revival hot-spots in more recent times also illustrate that it can happen in our time. I have personally been a partaker of several wonderful moves of God. I witnessed incredible love flowing freely at the same time as amazing miracles were taking place. The love of God and the power of God were joined at the hip in these revivals. There is nothing like this powerful combination.

The gift of knowledge is our superior intelligence gathering agency or our CIA. The gift of wisdom trumps human wisdom every time. The gift of faith gives courage and produces miracles. Gifts of healings and miracles are signs and wonders that convince the unbeliever that God is real and working today. Prophecy is a great recruiting tool and is very useful in reenergizing weary warriors. It also reveals people's hearts to show them God's love. Discerning of spirits is another powerful weapon to uncover the wolves in sheep's clothing. The gift of tongues is like spiritual nutrition and exercise. It is used to build up our faith and edify our spirit. When combined with interpretation of tongues, it has the same power as prophesy.

Spiritual Ministries

God has also given the church special ministries, often called Five-Fold Ministries. They are specialists and have special assignments. The apostles are Kingdom "Master Builders" and army generals. Prophets keep us updated on messages from the throne of Heaven. Evangelists are gifted to take the good news everywhere. Pastors care for the needs of the sheep and lambs, healing and nurturing. Teachers dig deep into the Word of God and receive revelation and wisdom for saints of all ages.

PERSONAL CHECKUP TIME #13

1. Which spiritual fruit and gifts do you use the best or the most?

2. Which weapons would be most effective on your mountain?

3. How can you build greater unity with believers on your mountain?

4. Which of the five ministry gifts do you lean towards?

Chapter Seven

Onward and Upward

TAKING THE NEXT STEP

Up to this point we have focused on preparing our minds and hearts for the upward journey. We should by now more fully understand why it is so important to take our place as kings on one or more mountains of society. We should know how to keep our motives pure and how to use the gifts God has given us to take the mountain for Jesus.

But the time has come to move into action. How do we begin to press onward and upward? Here are some keys to moving forward.

A. Choose to not be complacent.

Determine in your heart that you are going forward regardless of opposition. You will not let complacency cool your zeal. You will carry the passion from the heart of Jesus and keep the fire hot by spending time fanning the flame of your zeal in His holy presence.

B. Look upward to a higher position on your mountain.

Do you have confidence that God will help you to the higher level? Begin to ask God for vision for the higher place for His glory. Visualize where that place might be and what God could accomplish with you on that higher place on your mountain.

C. Seek God for wisdom and miracles to get to next level.

Let God confirm your promotion with supernatural wisdom and miraculous events. Give God time to work things out perfectly. As James says, "Let patience have its perfect work that you may be perfect and complete, lacking nothing." (James 1:4)

D. Be bold and trust God when a higher door opens.

When a higher place becomes a possibility, don't let fear and panic have any place in your mind or heart. God has been preparing you for this and you can depend on Him to lead and guide you as you take your position for His glory.

FUNCTIONING IN THE HIGHER PLACE

A. Take a confident but increasingly humble attitude with you.

The higher you go, the more humility you will need to cope with the pressure. The temptation is always to feel more superior to those below you, but you must remember how you got to the higher place. It was through the miraculous power of God and the humility that came through failure and brokenness and being in the presence of an all-powerful God. At the same time, be confident that God, Who began a good work in you, will finish what He started. You have a mission and it's not about manifesting your own greatness, but about expanding His Kingdom.

B. Learn how you can best serve the people you now lead.

The higher you go, the more people you will have to serve, and your serving skills need to grow. You won't have favor with God or man without the heart of a servant. This is an indispensable key for success.

C. Keep priorities right.

When you move into a new position, your natural instinct will be to devote all your energies to prove yourself worthy of that position. It is very easy to change your priorities and forget your most important relationships.

Of course, you may have to spend more time working for a time, but remember that your relationship and intimacy with God is your top priority and your source of all wisdom and anointing. Secondly, your family still needs your love and leadership, whether you are male or female, and you must give them some of your time as well.

D. Don't get discouraged or defeated by mistakes or setbacks.

You can't expect to function on a new and higher level without making mistakes as a rookie. People expect you to make mistakes, and they will be watching how you react to your mistakes more than whether you make them or not. If you try to excuse your mistakes or appear to be in denial, you will lose respect. If you humble yourself and apologize, you will keep that respect.

If setbacks occur in spite of your good efforts, humble yourself and seek God for more wisdom. He is training you to depend on Him. Without setbacks, you might get too self-confident and forget to ask Him for the extra help you need.

Setbacks are character training for the next level. Remember, you are not going to settle in your new position – you are just camping. But you are committed to serving with all your heart while you are at that position. At any rate, the lessons you learn from your failures will be invaluable when you go to the next level. Learn the skills and acquire the knowledge you need as quickly as possible and prepare to move to an even higher place on the mountain.

E. Don't get comfortable.

God needs kings at all positions of the mountain, including the very top. You might have everything you want for personal and family satisfaction, but God doesn't. He wants more influence on your mountain. So look upward again and pray for higher doors to open to you.

At the same time, keep tabs on your motives and dedicate every day to God's purpose and His Kingdom. Keep seeking God for a deeper place of intimacy. Ask Him for more anointing on your spiritual gifts and more spiritual fruit in your life.

Do your best in your present position, but begin to explore ways in which to train yourself for a higher position. You may need to take computer courses or get some mentoring from a top expert in your field. Seek God for the best way to prepare for a higher calling.

F. Look up and learn from people already in the higher place.

Learn first what biblical principles they are following. Most success comes from following principles that God has given us in His word. The book of Proverbs is full of them, but you can find them all throughout the Bible. These include diligence, honoring others, listening to lowly people and children as well as royalty.

Secondly, learn what unbiblical things they are doing. Some temporary success does come to those who violate godly principles. These dishonest methods contain seeds of destruction and should be avoided like the plague.

PERSONAL CHECKUP TIME #14

1. Do you struggle with complacency?

2. Do you stay humble when promoted?

3. Can you visualize yourself in a higher place for the Kingdom of Heaven?

4. Who could be a role model for you? Whose life excites you the most?

5. Are you ready to take the next step upward?

6. Can you see any doors opening?

7. Will you go through them when they do?

Chapter Eight

Maximizing Your Influence

Each of us has only one life on earth to give to Jesus to build His Kingdom here. How can we live our lives in such a way that we can maximize our life energy to accomplish this goal? There are at least two key strategies that I would recommend to all those who already have some experience on the mountain where God has positioned them.

BECOMING SPIRITUAL FATHERS, MOTHERS AND MENTORS

At some point in your journey, as you reach a certain stage of maturity, which can't be defined by age, you will find your greatest impact will come not from your own particular ministry or career efforts, but from mentoring and encouraging others to follow in your footsteps. Ultimately your goal, in keeping with the whole tenor of this book, is to raise up as many Kingdom-minded "Mountain Climbers" as possible to not only duplicate what you are doing, but to surpass you in every way.

Our own purpose and delight is to raise up and train as many hundreds and thousands as possible to go far beyond our successes in ministry. Our whole focus in the final quarter or so of our lives is to be a spiritual father and mother to the younger generation and launch them into incredible Kingdom assignments.

A. Develop your mentoring talents

Every father or mother, grandfather or grandmother has a certain amount of natural instinct when it comes to loving and mentoring their kids and grandkids, but many skills can be greatly improved upon by seeking more wisdom from God and other men and women of God. Our goal is to give you a few first steps in this process.

My first suggestion is to increase or supplement the love instinct and decrease of diminish the critical or judgmental instinct we all have as we age. There are many things that the younger generation likes and does that go against our own traditions, and they will constantly push us out of our comfort zone. I certainly can speak from experience on this.

Music is a primary example. What is music to one person may sound like torment to another. What I used to preach boldly from the pulpit is no longer what I believe or practice. God had to expose a religious spirit in me and deliver me from it.

The attitude and freedom of expression regarding sex and morals may also come as a shock to our systems. As with music, God will often use our own children to expose our own wrong and "religious" attitudes.

The lack of what we would call "good character" in areas such as being tidy, organized, on time and courteous may tend to make us reject the younger person on our mountain. But at the same time, we may not appreciate the amazing sensitive spirit and loving compassion they possess for others. They may have more spiritual fruit such as love, joy and peace than we do, but we tend to reject them if they don't abide by our standards of character.

A second suggestion is that we speak prophetically into as many younger lives as we possibly can. Just as criticism has turned many younger people away from the older generation, prophetic encouragement will draw them back to a place of honor and respect for the older generation.

When we focus on giving them vision and positive affirmation of their destiny, we will find ourselves attracted to certain ones and they will find themselves attracted to us. These are the ones we will probably find ourselves discipling. These are the ones we can help position on their mountain. Naturally, we will be most effective mentoring those who are called to the same mountain as we have been on.

A third suggestion is that we focus on just a few at the beginning, but that we give them some quality time and some tangible show of support. This could be taking them with us to important events or supporting them financially in specialized training. Above all, we need to let them know that we believe in them and that they are special to us and to God's Kingdom. We will tell them that they are called to rule on the Mountain of the Lord with other leaders.

B. Join with other mountain leaders to facilitate Kingdom expansion strategy.

When you are already on a high place on your mountain, you will want to make strategic alliances with other top-level leaders, both on your own mountain and on the other mountains of society. Your influence and impact can be far greater if you join forces with other Kingdom commanders.

On your own mountain, you must resist the temptation for competition with other leaders. You are on the same team and must keep Heaven's priorities, not your own. But you must also connect with leaders on other mountains and increase the influence and impact of all mountains.

For instance, leaders from every other mountain of society need to be in touch with leaders on the finance mountain for the projects God calls them to. They also need to be in constant communication with leaders on the religion mountain to keep up with what the apostles and prophets of the Lord are hearing from Heaven regarding the church and the world.

Leaders on the government mountain need to work with leaders on the media mountain. Without media support, achieving political objectives will be a very difficult task.

Another great partnership would be when the leaders of the education and entertainment mountains begin working together in a serious way. Multitudes of young people get most of their information from the entertainment mountain, and educators should make use of entertainers to convey information in a more creative way.

The family mountain is radically influenced by the government and the entertainment mountain. Regulations and definitions relating to marriage, divorce, discipline, abortion, etc., by various arms of government have tremendous impact on families in our society. And remember that movies, TV programs, popular music and other artistic expressions can be life-giving or devastating to the traditional family.

We could go on and on, but I'm sure we all get the point. We need to work for a spirit of unity and value the impact of the other mountains. Our natural tendency is to feel that our mountain is far more important than any other. It's time to pursue unity at this level and work together for the Kingdom of Heaven, by combining our little kingdoms for the glory of the King of kings.

PERSONAL CHECKUP TIME #15

1. Are you in a mentoring relationship now with anyone?

2. What examples do you know from Scripture of good mentors?

3. What examples do you see in your world of mentoring relationships?

4. Do you see examples of people from different mountains working in unity?

5. Can you think of other mountain combinations for Kingdom advantage?

Ben R. Peters

With over 40 years of ministry experience, Ben Peters with his wife, Brenda, have been called to an international apostolic ministry of equipping and activating others. As founders and directors of Open Heart Ministries, Ben and Brenda have ministered to tens of thousands with teaching and prophetic ministry. The result is that many have been saved, healed, delivered and activated into powerful ministries of their own.

Ben has been given significant insights for the body of Christ and has written fourteen books in the past ten years, since beginning a full-time itinerant ministry. His passions and insights include unity in the body of Christ, accessing the glory of God, five-fold team ministry, prophetic ministry, and signs and wonders for the world-wide harvest.

Kingdom Sending Center
P.O. Box 25
Genoa, IL 60135

www.KingdomSendingCenter.org
ben.peters@kingdomsendingcenter.org

Books by Ben R. Peters

Kings and Kingdoms:
Anointing a New Generation of Kings
to Serve the King of Kings

Holy Passion—Desire on Fire:
Igniting the Torch of Godly Passion

Prophetic Ministry: Strategic Key to the Harvest

Resurrection! A Manual for Raising the Dead

Signs and Wonders—To Seek or Not to Seek:
Exploring the Power of the Miraculous
to Bring People to Faith in God

With Me: A Captivating Journey Into Intimacy

Catching Up to the Third World:
Seven Indispensable Keys to Explosive Revival
in the Western Church

Folding Five Ministries Into One Powerful Team:
Taking the Prophetic and Apostolic Reformation
to the Next Powerful Level

God Ahead, Be So Emotional:
Empowering the Emotional Personality
to do Awesome Exploits for God

God's Favorite Number:
The Secret Keys and Awesome Power of True Unity

Birthing the Book Within You:
Inspiration and Practical Help
to Produce Your Own Book

Kings and Kingdoms
Anointing a New Generation of Kings
to Serve the King of Kings
by Ben R. Peters

Holy Passion: Desire on Fire
Igniting the Torch of Godly Passion
by Ben R. Peters

With Me
A Captivating Journey Into Intimacy
by Ben R. Peters

Available from Kingdom Sending Center
www.kingdomsendingcenter.org

Resurrection!
A Manual for Raising the Dead
by Ben R. Peters

Available from Kingdom Sending Center
www.kingdomsendingcenter.org

Prophetic Ministry
Strategic Key to the Harvest
by Ben R. Peters

Signs and Wonders
To Seek or Not to Seek
by Ben R. Peters

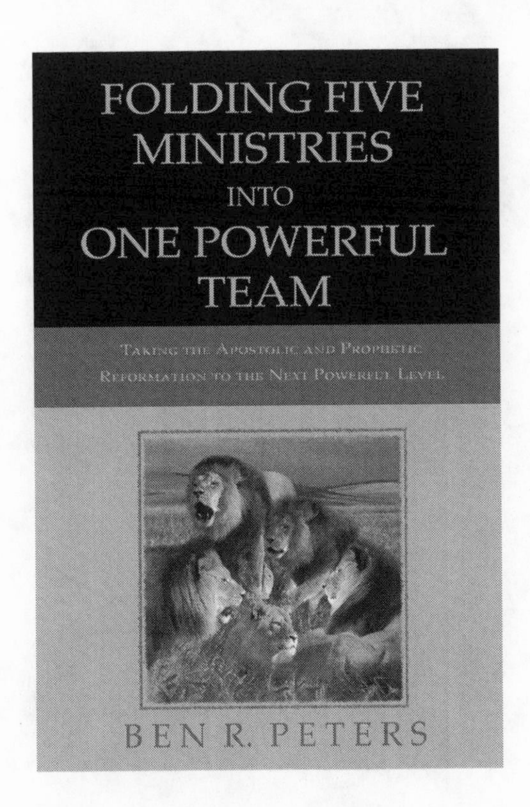

Folding Five Ministries Into
One Powerful Team

Taking the Apostolic and Prophetic Reformation
to the Next Powerful Level
by Ben R. Peters

Go ahead,
BE SO
EMOTIONAL
Empowering the Emotional
Personality To do Awesome
Exploits for God
BEN R. PETERS

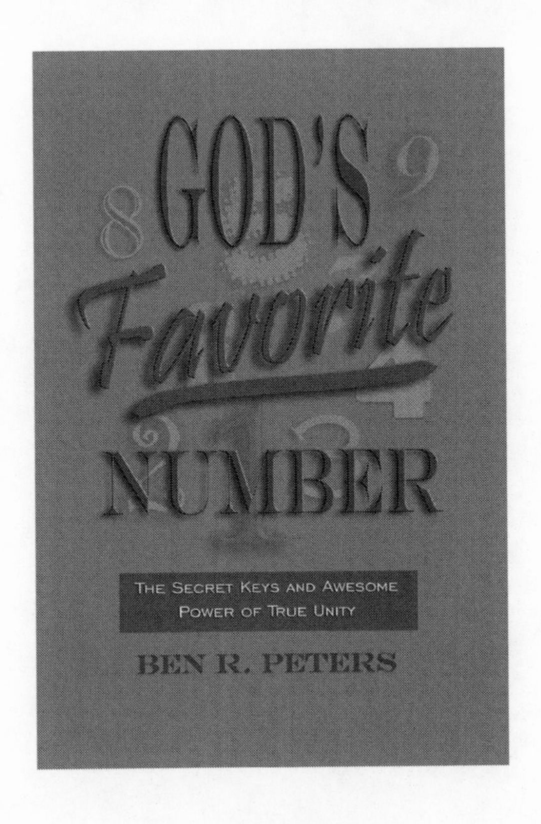

God's Favorite Number
The Secret Keys and Awesome
Power of True Unity
by Ben R. Peters

Catching Up
to the
Third World
Seven Indispensable Keys
To EXPLOSIVE Revival
In the Western Church
BEN R. PETERS

God Is So God!
The Adventures of a Traveling Ministry
on a Prophetic Faith Journey
by Brenda Peters

The Skin & the Skeleton
What to Do When the Laid-Back
Marries the Up-Set
by Ken Peters

Birthing the Book Within You
Inspiration and Practical Help
to Produce Your Own Book
by Ben R. Peters

Made in the USA
Charleston, SC
08 May 2012